Introduction to the history of China

The development from 1900 until today

by Annemarie Laurenz

Table of Contents

I. Collapse of the Empire

Traditional China begins to disintegrate in the mid-19th century. The western world enters the great land under the imperial **Qing Dynasty**. So far, Chinese goods have been in great demand in England, France, and the United States, without China receiving goods in return from the West. Above all, the Chinese received silver as payment for tea, porcelain and other Far Eastern goods. There was an imbalance in the trade relationship, against which, especially the English proceeded. They brought opium to China. Here, this was used as medicine, but also resulted in dangerous addiction. When China went against these imports, the **Opium War (1840-1842)** took place. The English won because of their military and technical superiority. The Chinese military was very poorly equipped, simple soldiers and generals ran away without a fight.

China had to sign the **Treaty of Nanking,** which had many drawbacks. The worst part of it being that it had to cede the island of Hong Kong to England. China was also forced to open five of the largest ports, so that the British could now legally import opium and other Western goods into China. In addition, the English were now allowed to acquire property in China. They were allowed to evangelize and built a religious and philosophical Christian doctrine in direct opposition to the teachings of Confucius, which formed the basis for the world view of the Chinese.

Political bases were built. Besides England, France and the USA also installed their Embassies in Beijing (later, Russia also followed). These two powers also imposed contracts on China, in which China lost the right to levy customs duties. Now, numerous goods arrived permanently in China from abroad, which strained the domestic economy.

China had become, to a great extent, a colonial area of the western world.

At that time, the Chinese lived largely on agriculture and crafts. Many farmers helped themselves to additional income by spinning and weaving. Over time, they began to sell yarn and cotton in the cities. They contested the excessive tax fees on their profit. Business and pre-industrial production also continued to develop in urban areas. Small businesses were established, making various pieces of furniture. In addition, textile production along with paper and shoe production evolved.

As the urban population grew, many Chinese worked in these types of businesses, but were poorly paid. Due to these conditions, English and other western goods came into the market.

Imports now interfere with the development of their own productions, especially since taxes are due on domestic businesses, but not on foreign imports. The fabrics from England and other goods are made with much better and more complex machines. Therefore, making it difficult for the Chinese to compete with their own products. But not only the owners of industrial small businesses are pressurized. The craft enterprises, not to mention the dealers, are threatened in their existence or have significant losses. The factory workers receive increasingly lower wages. The large number of farmers also becomes depleted as leases rise.

Overall, living and working conditions in China worsen drastically for large parts of the population. At the same time, we have the imperial court, the aristocrats and the well-earning officials.

With Western economic conditions, Western ideas also come to China. Especially the educated elite start to consider another form of government. There are **models such as democracy and socialism**. The younger generation of higher social classes can no longer expect to automatically reach the same position as their parents. Children of civil servants, generals, factory owners, traders and landowners see the foreign powers as the enemies of their future. They are progressively inclined to believe that the Qing Dynasty was

the last of its kind. China should become a
republic.

5

**Due to the economic conditions on one
hand, and the radical theories they were
dealing with on the other, the tremen-
dous upheaval of twentieth century is
explained.**

II. Boxer Rebellion

At the end of the 19th century, natural catastrophes hit different layers of impoverished populations. In 1998, the Yangtze River's shores overflowed for months, causing huge floods that left millions of Chinese people homeless and leaving more than $20 billion in economic damage.

Now, forces were formed, directed against the foreign powers and against the Christians. The result was a coalition called **"The Righteous and Harmonious Fists,"** to which farmers in particular belonged. The Western press described this as the **"Boxer"**. Namely due to its members practicing various martial arts, including boxing, and other physical rituals. Their goal was to drive all foreigners out of their country and eliminate the Chinese Christians who had been proselytized. They regarded these two groups as the root of social evil.

In 1899, the Boxers attacked Christian missionaries and practicing Christians, and in 1900 they fought foreign merchants in a major uprising, especially in Beijing.

For this, they were supported by the **Empress Dowager Cixi**. She was the widow of Emperor Xianfeng and had taken over the rule of the empire after his death in 1861. The Europeans regarded them as "white barbarians" and therefore, supported the **Boxer Rebellion**, as it is called later in history. She ordered the killing of all foreigners. Many foreign envoys and their families fall victim to the massacre.

The rebellion was crushed. Under the leadership of England, an alliance was formed with France, Italy, Austria-Hungary, Germany, Japan, USA and Russia, who sent their troops to China to put an end to the Boxer Rebellion.

In the following years, China is shaken by numerous unrests and local rebellions.

III. Formation of the Republic of China

After the Boxer Rebellion, the aristocratic Qing dynasty issued Empress Cixi with some reforms. Economically, they should be used to promote the development of Chinese enterprises, and in domestic terms, education and a fairer justice system were strengthened. The worst conditions, namely slavery, the widespread opium consumption and the foot binding of women (little girls' toes would be broken, and their feet were tied together and crippled to fit the ideal of beauty)were banned.

But the stipulations were not enough for many people, especially as they were not consistently implemented. This formed resistance to the Empire. Cixi died in 1908. Formally, the new ruler was the two-year-old descendant **Puyi**, who is housed in the Forbidden City as a child Emperor, while two other adult descendants take power. (The **Forbidden City** was the center of Beijing, where the imperial court was located until 1911, and only high-ranking personalities had access).

In May 1911, the Qing dynasty announced that it would transfer two railway lines from private to state ownership. This sparked big **protests in the Sichuan province**, where many investors were involved in the railways, which now joined forces as a countermovement and organized strikes. The protest was crushed; at least 40 died. Although the government paid higher compensation after this, the morale changed and became critical of the regime.

Officers, soldiers, students and workers started meeting in secret where they would read revolutionary texts and set up an arsenal. On October 9th, 1911, a bomb accidentally exploded in a meeting place in Wuchang, the capital of the Hubei province. Anti-government critics were, thus, discovered and arrested. In response, the rebels raided and occupied the provincial government headquarters the next day.

They proclaimed the Republic and set up a flag with 18 stars. Hence, a union of all China was to be represented as a republic consisting of 18 Qing specified provinces.

The takeover of the government immediately led to similar rebellions in other provinces. Independence from the Qing dynasty was proclaimed throughout the country. At first, this was done with little violence, but the intervention of the state power led to fierce fighting and many deaths. The government succeeded in recapturing several provincial capitals, including Wuchang.

The Qing government was now virtually finished. But this great empire, it was not possible to simply replace it with another government that could handle all 18 provinces. Most provinces had proclaimed their independence, but their new governments had very different ideas. A common idea was to unite China into a republic.

Historically, the year 1912 is considered the founding year for the Republic of China. But the years up until 1949, when the official end of the Republic of China came, became chaotic.

The most important factors are shown next.

IV. Sun Yat-sen and Yuan Shikai

1. Sun Yat-sen

Sun Yat-sen was born in 1866 as a farmer's son. His youth was marked by a difficult life of high taxes and hard work, and he devoted himself to ideas of a better social life. He also studied medicine abroad. Early on, he joined secret societies, which had in mind the abolishment of the Qing dynasty, and which founded several groups. They aimed for a national association of the provinces in a republic. In 1905, he founded a political organization called **Tongmenhui**, which incorporated several national movements. At the same time, he overwhelmed the government with his petitions calling for political reform.

Tongmenhui is responsible for several riots, which all fail. The young doctor has to flee China because of his involvement. He continues to study revolutionary theories, such as the French Revolution and the American

Revolutionary War. He summarizes his revolutionary ideas in scriptures, and ensures that they are spread throughout China.

His popularity causes him to return from abroad in 1911 and become the **leader of the revolution**. When the country is declared Republic of China on January 1, 1912, he becomes the first president. China is given a provisional constitution and uses the US as a republic as its model. He rules in progressive Nanking, but he has no military to fall back on. Therefore, in 1912, he relinquishes his position of power to the military leader and supporter of the Qing, **Yuan Shikai**. He offers to become president if in return he abolishes imperial rule and supports the new republic. Yuan takes on the presidency, but then opposes Sun.

In 1912, Sun made the political party **Kuomintang** from the Tongmenhui Association. Sometime later, he succeeds in establishing a republican government in Guangzhou, the capital of the Guangdong province, with the help of a military leadership. The fruits of his political labour, however, remain limited to southern areas of China.

In the last few years before his death from cancer in 1925, he dedicated his time to specifying his ideas for a reform. He summarized his ideas in three principles: **nationalism, democracy and national prosperity.**

Above all, he understood **nationalism** to mean the end of the Qing dynasty. He also wanted to combat the supremacy of the ethnic group of the Manchuria, who were strongly represented in the government and dominated China. He wanted to see the great Han ethnic group as a national entity. The fact that the Manchurian rulers had determined the fate of all China in the Qing dynasty for decades, they made visible through their hairstyle. They ordered the wearing of the "Queue" for all men. With the outbreak of the revolution in 1911, the Han cut their braids and thus showed the sign of their oppression. Sun believed that a united China with democratic leadership would automatically be recognized by the Western states.

To establish a **democracy**, he wanted to proceed step by step. First, military units should ensure law and order. Then elections should be held, and parliaments should be established so that a representative body would emerge.

Under the representation of the people, the large landowners were taxed more heavily and the farmers who leased the land from them were relieved. In this way, he believed he would avoid an escape from the countryside to the city. His philosophy was that if the poor did not work in urban enterprises for little money, no poor working class would develop like in the western world. That is how **national prosperity** should arise.

However, his fellow campaigners had a different view that was later adopted in the Communist Party. It included the complete expropriation of wealthy landowners.

Sun Yat-sen is still revered by both China and Taiwan as its founding father.

2. Yuan Shikai

Yuan Shikai was Sun's opponent. He was born in 1859 as the son of a middle-class family. Early on, he rises in the government and army. As military leader and politician of the Qing, he accepted Sun's offer to become president of the Chinese Republic in 1912. He promotes the ousting of the Qing, by forcing the child Emperor Puyi to resign, thus neutralizing his imperial representatives.

But then, he works against the republican movement and the Kuomintang, which gained a strong position in the National Assembly in 1913. He sees to it that Beijing is the capital instead of the Republican Nanking.

Before the new republican institutions could develop, he disempowered them again. Sun launched an attack on him in 1913, but he cannot do anything against him and his military.

Shikai works on the reintroduction of the monarchy until 1916. He dissolves the National Assembly. Then he gives in to the various demands of Japan. Among them, especially the admission that the Japanese received considerable control over Manchuria, was incomprehensible to many Chinese people. When he finally tries to bring himself to the throne, large protests are held. Yuan dies in 1916, leaving unrest and anything but a united China.

V. Development of the Kuomintang party

The Kuomintang is founded in August 1912 as a result of the Tongmenghui and other national-thinking groups joining forces.

It is a political party that wants to be represented in the National Assembly. This parliament is a result of the revolution, and is newly created. While the **National Assembly** emerges through elections that represent progress from Qing rule, the electoral process is far from democratic. Only male voters (aged 21 and over) who are landowners are allowed to go to the polls. Alternatively, men who can show any kind of education are also allowed to vote. In total, between 5 and 6 percent of the total population who were allowed to vote came together in this way. For their part, however, they voted for electors who ultimately determined their participation in parliament. Therefore, a lot of corruption was at play.

The president of Kuomintang is **Song Jiaoren**. **Sun Yat-sen**, on the other hand, is the member who is considered a spiritual father. In the **National Assembly in 1913**, the party receives about 45 percent of the seats. But the parliament turns out to be helpless in dealing with the new political ideas of a democratic republic. It has no experience, and the population is critical as well as suspicious. People argue a lot and constantly think about how to handle power. In addition, Yuan Shikai works hard against the new parliament (the National Assembly). He has already achieved that it will be moved from Nanking to Beijing. When his political enemy, Song Jiaoren, is murdered, he is suspected to be the reason for his death.

When Sun loses his rebellion against Shikai in the same year, he has to flee abroad, and the party loses its members and influence. At the end of 1913, Shikai managed to expel the members of the Kuomintang from the government and dissolve the National Assembly.

Sun turns to the **Soviet Union** and receives their support. He now builds the Kuomintang into a militaristic party with revolutionary ideas, and introduces stronger hierarchy and discipline.

After Shikai's death, the party systematically builds a strong military wing. Through this, Sun and his colleagues succeed in forming a militaristic republican government in the Guangdong province.

In the 1920s, Sun founds the **Whampoa Military Academy**, which trains soldiers and officers especially. From it, many graduates emerge, who strengthen the **National Revolutionary Army**, as they strengthened, and through provincial armies, they expanded Kuomintang Army is called. But the co-existing Communist Party benefits from the training at the Academy. Sun also works with it on the advice of the Soviet Union.

The Kuomintang combines many political currents at Sun's death. When the charismatic leader dies, he leaves a big gap and conflicting points of view. The Soviets, the Chinese Communists as well as the **Comintern**, but also individual **warlords** of the southern provinces had influenced it over time.

The **Communist International, often referred in short as the Comintern**, was an organization in which the communist parties of the world had joined forces. It was founded in 1919 at the instigation of the Russian revolutionary leader Lenin. Their goal was the world revolution, carried by the working class.

The **warlords** were dukes of war who dominated individual regions in the turmoil of fragmented China after the death of Shikai from 1916 to 1927. It was a group of very different leaders. They all used military means for their rule, but they had opposing views. Some did not want to give up on the Qing dynasty, others wanted a new national China. Some only sought land ownership, with the hope of eventually forming their own government with themselves positioned at the top.

The warlords were known for their ruthless enrichment. They controlled their territories and the peasant and artisanal enterprises on them, imposed high taxes and violently enforced them. In addition, they caused the population to grow opium again, and make it freely available for sale. Their armies stole what they liked from private possessions. The warlords printed large amounts of money to pay their soldiers; which led to high inflation. Above all, the peasantry suffered under their unpredictable rulers. Few warlords were interested in social reform. The national government that had established itself in Beijing was partly under the control of the warlords, and thus, were the foreign trade tariffs and the tax revenues that converged there.

VI. The May Fourth Movement

The **May FourthMovement of 1919** refers to a student protest that ignited from the Treaty of Versailles. It provided that China had to cede the Shandong Province to Japan. But the spiritual roots for the student uprising are deeper. In 1910, the New Cultural Movement was founded, whose followers wanted to transform China into a democracy. Disappointed by the 1911 revolution, the members continued to meet.

They wanted a Western-style liberal country, with the intellectual group attaching great importance to advances in science. The Chinese conventions, especially the teaching of Confucius should be overcome. People wanted to achieve equality between people, and here, the first demands for the equality of women were made.

More than 3,000 demonstrators; mostly students, met in Tiananmen Square in Beijing on May 4th, demanding the government not to sign the Treaty of Versailles. The demonstration was dissolved and over 30 participants arrested. But a day later, not only the Beijingers, but also the students of other cities became active. They went on strike.

This triggered solidarity among the workers in Shanghai, a major city with a highly developed industry by Chinese standards.

They understood the concerns of the students, but they also had their own demands. Approximately 100,000 workers entered the general strike in June, which lasted several days. The participants demanded higher wages and better working conditions.

These events raised tensions in the country. In addition to the student body, workers and political groups openly expressed dissatisfaction with the government, which was no longer able to stand idly by. The government released the detained students, and let some of the more unwelcome members of the government go. The government also worked to ensure that the Treaty of Versailles was not ratified. However, they could not stop Shandong from being turned over to Japan.

After this movement, the radicalization of many sections of the population was unstoppable.

It is the breeding ground for the future founding of the Chinese Communist Party, especially since its long-time leader Mao Zedong experienced it. Large parts of China were no longer willing to support the existing conditions. The political groups; some of which were newly founded, no longer relied on foreign aid, but sought a self-determined path to another social order.

VII. The Communist Party of China

After the May Fourth Movement, groups based on European Marxism emerged. This did not only include political, but also literary groups with many writers.

They joined forces in 1921, and founded the Chinese Communist Party (CCP) in Shanghai.

There were only 12 people, including Mao Zedong. The salient leaders, however, were **Chen Duxiu** and **Li Dazhao**. The members believed in the communist theory of the European **Karl Marx**. Their current political role model was **Vladimir Lenin**, who led the Bolshevik revolution in Russia in 1917, which led to the founding of the communist Soviet Union.

This means they did not follow the ideas of a democratic republic based on the Western model, but took the Soviet Un-

ion as their example. They wanted to isolate themselves from the economic and political influence of other powers, unite China and abolish the exploitation of humans.

The party initially remained small and could not gain influence. In the first years after its founding, it barely had 1,000 members. They sought advice and help from Moscow, from where they were heavily controlled. The Comintern, which had its headquarters there, did not trust the CCP to act as a revolutionary party and to be taken seriously enough in China. Therefore, they were advised to associate with the Nationalist Party of China, the Kuomintang. Just as Moscow had influenced the Kuomintang, the CCP also received instructions from there. For example, in a 1922 telegram, the communists were supposed to form revolutionary cells in both the Kuomintang and the unions. In addition, the party should introduce more discipline and organize itself more professionally.

Under the control of Moscow, Kuomintang and the CCP worked together to create the **First United Front**, which existed from 1924 to 1927. Its goal was the reunification of China. However, since both parties had very opposing views on the forms of government and society that were supposed to reign in a unified China, there were many issues. Also, the question of where and how exactly one should proceed politically and militarily in order to achieve a change led to fundamental differences. However, the CCP got access to the Whampoa Military Academy, founded by Kuomintang leader Sun, and so its members acquired a great deal of military knowledge.

Over time, the CCP communists came to better understand that they needed to retain their members. To do this, they built up a counter-ideology to the family. The Chinese traditionally had an intense attachment to the extended family and their home village. The party acted decisively against this attitude and replaced the nation and a just state - which one wanted to establish - with family and ancestors.

VIII. Rebellion andmassacre in Shanghai

In 1927, there was a clash between the Kuomintang and CCP parties.

Part infighting developed within the Kuomintang. A left-wing Kuomintang government had established itself in Wuhan, and a right wing in Nanking. In early 1927, the Comintern, along with the CCP, initiated some rebellions in Shanghai, where workers also arose. In the process, they won a victory against the strong warlords. The two Kuomintang governments reacted differently to this. Leftist Wuhan leader **Wang Jingwei** supported the communist action, while the right-wing leader on Nanking's side, **Chiang Kai-shek**, did not accept the rebellion. Now, the right wing of the Kuomintang went so far as to launch a large-scale action against the communists. His aim was to keep the revolutionary communists out of the process of creating a unified China.

On April 12, under Chiang Kai-shek's leadership, the communists in Shanghai are severely attacked. In this, he is supported by a criminal gang, called the **Green Gang**. All communists and their sympathizers who can be caught are arrested. The range goes from insurgent workers to party members, including those who were communists in the Kuomintang. Hundreds are rounded up and taken into custody. Most are officially sentenced to death; others are killed in the clashes. This extermination of the communists lasted for several weeks. After that, thousands of people are missing. This event is condemned by the later Communist Party as **White Terror**. Generally, this term identifies violent measures intended to suppress revolutionary movements.

With the attack on the communists in Shanghai, Chiang Kai-shek prevented a CCP government in the important industrial area of Shanghai.

The party was severely weakened. Many members fled or went underground. Several avoided the areas in which the Kuomintang ruled, and settled in the country where the Nationalist Party had no influence.

The united front between the Kuomintang and the CCP was now broken.

The Soviets stopped their relief efforts for the Kuomintang. The CCP was forced to reassess itself. The Shanghai massacre is generally seen as the beginning of the **Chinese Civil War**, which historically dates from **1927 to 1949**. Chiang Kai-shek was one of its main characters.

IX. Chiang Kai-shek

Chiang Kai-shek was born in 1887 as the son of a well-to-do merchant. Early on, he was interested in politics and military. He became a member of Sun's Tongmenghui. When Sun ceased to be leader of the Kuomintang because of his early death, he became his successor. In the 1911 revolution, he made a name for himself as a military leader against the Qing dynasty. He also supported Sun and the Kuomintang in the attack against Yuan Shikaiin 1913. Because he was unsuccessful, he initially moved himself to Japan. He then returned, but remained underground. Here, he built a close connection to the Green Gang, which had evolved from a patriotic connection of boatmen on inland waters to a part of the organized crime which dominated the opium trade among others. These gang members later help him with the Shanghai massacre.

Chiang is an excellent, well trained military commander. In 1924, he became commander of the Whampoa Military Academy and in

1926, commander-in-chief of the **National Revolutionary Army**, which consists of about 100,000 soldiers. With them, he can successfully fight the particularly ruthless warlords who terrorize the people of northern China. That brings him respect and trust. A year later, he defeats the Shanghai Uprising, and in the following years, he repeats his attacks on the communists. He despises them as vassals of Moscow.

Before, it had been unclear for a long time what political line he followed against the communists. With the Shanghai Massacre, he initiated the final separation from them.

In 1928, Chiang Kai-shek beat or sidelined much of the warlords in north and east China. The renewed success brings him the post of State Council. His **government based in Nanking** is nationally oriented. He seeks contact with large landowners, who also support him because of his anti-communist views. For the intellectual elite, he takes the standpoint of realizing the theory of Sun's three principles. He proclaims that now the stage of democracy is reached and the government, with military units, can ensure law and order before elections and a representative body can become reality. To strengthen the personality cult, he has Sun's corpse housed in a huge mausoleum.

He becomes a strong man and president of China, which he was able to reunite in good part in the 1920s. In 1949, he flees to Taiwan because the communists seize power.

Under Chiang Kai-shek, in the years 1928 to 1937, in terms of Chinese conditions, there was a relatively quiet period of time. The governor wants to build a republic and a politically reliable system. The reunification of China is set to advance. He governs with the **national Kuomintang party in the capital Nanking**. The Western world believes that it pursues innovative policies, embraces Western values and promotes China's economy. But abroad, one does not notice that many provincial areas in the large country are not covered by the Kuomintang. Here, the old conditions still prevail, and often, the warlords still have their say. The desired economic growth develops only partially.

The government also has a big problem of not being recognized everywhere, even if it is on site. The population, accustomed to centuries of imperial dynasties, questions the authority of a new government. The government officials cannot control everything that happens in the country. There is still a lot of corruption, and above all, a pronounced opium trade. For this reason, the Kuomintang becomes more militaristic over time. It also has no experience in governing a giant empire and still bases its financial management on old practices. So, it tries to implement reforms by the civil service, but this often fails.

Chian Kai-shek was a highly disciplined man, meticulously attentive to his appearance and always in control of his behaviour. He appeared in impeccable uniform, which he liked to decorate with medals, and in expensive civilian clothes. Even when angry, he practiced self-restraint. Quite different is his adversary, who built a mass movement in the years he was China's leading politician, namely **Mao Zedong**. The opponent appeared in the worn blue clothes of the farmers as well as a red guard hat. When he talked to people, he approached them and showed great interest in them. This made an excellent way to build trust.

X. Mao Zedong

Mao Zedong was born in 1893 to the son of a well-to-do farmer. Although the family does not go hungry, he is confronted with natural disasters and as a result, famine in his homeland, the Hunan Province. The **great famine in 1910** lays the foundation for his joining the 1911 anti-Qing movement. One of his first political actions was to emulate the insurgents of the revolution and to cut off his fellow students' braids without asking them, which were seen as a sign of oppression. Mao earns his living as a librarian and teacher.

He is an extremely diligent reader and educates himself through books. Most especially, historical and political topics captivate him. He knows many literary works, but he also knows the **Communist Manifesto of Karl Marx**. Finally, he goes on to write his own scripts. In 1919, he goes to Beijing, after he develops great sympathy for the May FourthMovement. There he manages to publish his papers on the development of trade unions and even on women's rights. He now gets to know some communists.

In July 2021, he is one of the founding members of the CCP. In his home province of Hunan, he immediately starts campaigning for members of the party and building a CCP cell.

For this reason, he continues to publish his writings in which Marxist ideas can already be found. But Mao does not remain a theorist. He helps organize strikes and develops a close political relationship with workers in the textile, mining and rail industries, and establishes at least 20 different unions. He is keen to bring education to the workers and farmers, and he provides evening schools that offer various subjects, including the Chinese written language. Mao also uses this opportunity to spread his revolutionary views.

Mao followed the Soviet's instructions to support the Kuomintang and ended up joining the party, where he soon became the chief propagandist.

But after the death of Sun, and under the succession of Chiang Kai-shek he lost influence. He now devotes himself to the military training of farmers in Hunan.

In 1927, comes the decisive turning point in Mao's life. After the Shanghai massacre, the United Front becomes history; the Kuomintang and the CCP have become enemies. Mao is now working hard to mobilize the farmers, so that they can prevail against the warlords as well as against the Kuomintang. He has a strong ally with commander Zhu De, and can set up a militia. One of his great role models is the Soviet Union, and he has connections with the Comintern.

In 1927, he organizes the so-called Autumn Harvest Uprising to develop soviet farmers.

These were districts in which the worker and soldier councils of the Soviet Union had joined together and then passed into administrative units.

But the National Revolutionary Army prevented the project. Mao had to retreat to the
mountains for some time with Zhu De and his
troops. They then settle in the border provinces of Jiangxi and Fujian. Here, they founded the **Jiangxi Sovietin 1930**, a communist
community based on the Soviet model. They
now have their military base, and a regional
location for their squads.

**The result is the Jiangxi Soviet Republic,
officially called the Chinese Soviet Republic, which is kept until 1934.**

Mao's troops are the **Red Army** now, and
total more than 150,000 soldiers. There is
training in militant combat and guerrilla
methods as well as the possibility to manufac-
ture ammunition in their own production fa-
cility. This communist base is so strong that
the head of the CCP moves its headquarters
to Jiangxi.

**Many people had to give their lives for
this level of development, because Mao
had had all those who did not accept his**

leadership role executed at the end of 1930.

That counted for at least 10,000 people, but possibly hundreds of thousands more. The estimates vary widely. In addition, he did not hesitate to torture the women of real or alleged enemies to obtain information. Historians point out the two faces of Mao in this context. On the one hand, he was a fervent worshipper of freedom and justice and a staunch fighter for the oppressed, on the other, he was a tyrannical ruler and merciless dictator. That would be confirmed several times throughout history.

Mao Zedong himself now faces pressure. Now that the top party leadership is in the immediate vicinity, fundamental differences emerge. The party still shares the ideological attitude of the Comintern and the Soviet Union, and relies on the working class. However, Mao believes, that farmers are the mainstay of a revolution in China. Even in military matters, they are not in agreement. Mao removes himself from his fellow party members. The renegade region does not stay hidden from Chiang Kai-shek.

42

The Kuomintang leader attacks the Chinese Soviet Republic five times.

Mao can hold off attacks with his Red Guards a total of four times, but then faces defeat. In 1934, Mao and his communist squad have to give up their base and flee. They embark on a very long march.

XI. The Long March

In October 1934, the communists set off for the march, which lasts for a year. The destination is Yan'an in the north, near a border area controlled by the Soviet Union. They take everything possible, from furniture and printing presses to weapons. The march, which runs over several stages, becomes a struggle for survival. 18 high mountains and 24 rivers have to be crossed. Hunger, diseases and natural events such as heavy snow storms burden the troops. 6,000 kilometers were only accessible by foot. Above all, however, warlords and Chiang Kai-shek's army were expected on the journey. Thousands of men were lost in the fight with these troops. The Red Army loses about 40,000 soldiers in **the battle of the Xiang River** alone in November, when Chiang attacks from the air.

Mao and the rest of his squad arrive in Yan'an, located in the Shaanxi Province on the Yellow River, in October 1935.

With 15,000 men, about 10 percent of his fellow soldiers have survived.

By military standards, this is considered a defeat. Mao, however, manages to present the march as a heroic communist epic. In retrospect, he turns it into a propaganda campaign and proclaims that he was able to introduce the oppressed people to his Red Army in the 11 provinces that were crossed. He presents the attacks of Chiang Kai-shek on the Chinese Soviet Republic as a failure. He communicates the catastrophic loss of lives as heroic deeds of courageous communists.

The "Long March" becomes a legend that has a permanent place in the ideology of the CCP. Later on, even a rocket is named after it.

When the extended Politburo of the Chinese Communist Party meets in Zunyi in early 1935, Mao manages to blame the defeat on, amongst others, the military leader Otto Braun. He himself becomes a **member of the secretariat in the Politburo**. In addition, he makes his aim clear that no proletarian revolution, as in the Soviet Union, can apply to Chinese communism. The position of the nationalists under Chiang is established as the wrong path. Mao is on the way to power.

In Yan'an, Mao becomes increasingly better at realizing his claims to power. The glorified story of the "Long March" becomes an almost inexplicable powerful foundation for his personal recognition. Mao seeks to mobilize the masses, especially the farmers, in order to bring the oppressed people to power, after a (farmer) revolution. In addition, he wants to change the consciousness of the lower classes. He is able to appeal to the farmers with these views, as they still suffer from corruption and high tax burdens. This time in Yan'an is a crucial era in which Mao can improve his position and expand his theory.

In the years 1941 to 1944, Mao does everything to enforce and eliminate his opponents within the party.

First, he builds groups in which his writings are studied. Then he convinces the party members to reflect their own convictions, and if they deviate from his ideas to openly criticize themselves. Thus, the element of self-criticism is introduced. Mao understands that attitudes need to be corrected, as his leadership is not endorsed by all party members. Many of his allies are still convinced of the Soviet model which follows proletarian revolution. Mao now specifically pursues studies of his opponents due to his own belief in self-criticism. He introduces purges in which political dissidents are tortured and executed. Many committed suicide. At the end of 1944, there were about 10,000 deaths as a result of this campaign. Mao announces this era as a renewal of the party.

XII. Influence of the China-Japan war

The **Second Sino-Japanese War of 1937 to 1945** had great influence on China's political development. As early as 1931, the Japanese succeeded in militarily invading Manchuria. Here, they developed a puppet state. For this, they used the last Qing emperor. This was the now adult but cold-faced child Emperor **Puyi**, who, driven by President Chiang Kai-shek, agreed to the demands of the Japanese. In 1933, Chiang recognized the region as a Japanese dominion under the guise of imperial rule.

In mid-1937, the Japanese invaded northern China, to which they were far superior in terms of weapons technology. In the following two years, they occupied the east coast of China. They gained a sad notoriety for their particularly cruel treatment of prisoners of war and civilians. In the **massacre of Nanking,** they massacred approximately 300,000 people in the most brutal ways. They also used parts of China for experiments in biological and chemical warfare and carried out human experiments involving pathogens. They practiced the principle of scorched earth. In the wake of the Second World War in 1945, Japan however, had to capitulate in China, which it had occupied with about 1 million men.

Chiang Kai-shek was heavily criticized during and after the war because he gave the impression that he was more concerned with dealing with the communists than with the confrontation of the Japanese.

His government was now considered corrupt, and he could not solve the country's economic problems. Nevertheless, his government had to bear the brunt of the war.

Meanwhile, the CCP, with Mao, reorganized itself in the Yan'an Soviet. The number of its members rose to about 800,000. The Red Army defended northwestern China against the Japanese. The rural areas where the communists were represented, however, were largely spared of the attacks because the attackers concentrated their efforts on the cities. As a result, this gave the impression overseas and especially in the US, that the rural areas were successfully defended by Mao's CCP, while Chiang's Kuomintang failed. The CCP exploited this and presented itself to the foreign countries as a powerful party in China, which represented a real alternative to the government.

Thus, the war meant that Mao and his party had a great advantage over Chiang.

XIII. Second United Front

The relationship between the nationalists of the Kuomintang and the CCP has been problematic for many years, and after the end of the First United Front, certainly has not remained unencumbered. But Moscow (with the communist dictator Josef Stalin) and the Comintern repeatedly demanded that the communists work with non-communist governments to counter the Japanese. After that, the CCP turned. It created slogans like "Chinese should not fight against Chinese".

In 1936, the Second United Front between the CCP and the Kuomintang came into existence and lasted until 1946.

But, by their nature, it was essentially just a joint stance to ward off the Japanese. There was not even any cooperation between the nationalist Chiang troops and the Red Army, which was used more to engage in guerrilla warfare.

Chiang could not hide his hatred for the communists, saying that the Japanese were a skin disease, while the communists were a disease of the heart. In areas not threatened by the Japanese, the two Chinese armies actually fought each other.

In early 1941, nationalist Kuomintang units attacked the headquarters of the Red Army. They killed (or captured or abducted) more than 70 percent of the approximately 9,000 communists present.

After this heavy blow, the communists portrayed themselves as patriotic martyrs. It was not unknown outside of China that Chiang's interest lay heavily in the extermination of the communists, from which the CCP benefited. After the war, the two Chinese parties were enemies again.

XIV. Conflicts between Kuomintang and CCP

For foreign powers, especially the US, it was clear at the end of World War II that the civil war in China would continue. They would remain to be right.

Between 1945 and 1949, the main phase of the conflict between Kuomintang and the CCP unfolds. The opponents are Mao and Chiang.

When the war ends, disputes occur about who the war loser, Japan, should surrender to, the ruling Kuomintang, or the strong CCP. Then Mao and his longtime companion and comrade **Zhou Enlai** met on urgent advice from Moscow, with Chiang Kai-Shek and his colleagues to lead peace talks in the presence of an American diplomat. They take place in Chongqing, where the Kuomintang had its headquarters.

Here, both parties are willing to compromise and claim to want to work together. But that turns out to be a fake maneuver.

Behind each other's backs, both return to their own party and try to strengthen it. Additionally, both mobilize their own armies again.

The CCP had moved its base after the Japanese defeat in Manchuria. Chiang did not accept this. He negotiated with Moscow, which had troops located there, with the aim of being able to build a base there for his Kuomintang. The Soviets agreed to this, but they transported the Japanese Manchurian industrial plants to the Soviet Union, and at the same time provided Mao's Red Army with weapons and the spoils of the war.

As a result, the communist forces, which were strongly focused on guerrilla warfare, could become a well-equipped military force, especially as they also received military training through Moscow.

Further urging from the US to achieve a stable agreement between the two hardened party fronts failed. In 1947, American President **Harry Truman** angrily states that he sees extremist elements at work on both sides who only pursue their own interests.

The population was worsening in the years of civil war. The government was creating increasingly more debt. The war against Japan, the high expenditures for the military and the still existing high corruption rate took its toll. The party did not put backed money on the market, which led to extreme inflation. If you could still get a whole pig for 100 Yuan in 1940, three years later, you only got one chicken, two years later a fish, in the following year just an egg and after that the money was not even worth that anymore. This made the black market grow, and of course, many people started turning to crime.

Businesses could not grow, nor could new businesses be established, which increased the number of unemployed people immensely. The population be-

came increasingly dissatisfied with the Kuomintang government, and even the soldiers began to rebel against the system.

This got even worse when Chiang blew up part of the Yellow River to divide the opposing forces. The resulting flood hit several hundred villages, and several hundred thousand people lost their homes.

The CCP, on the other hand, was becoming increasingly popular. Although Chiang succeeded in conquering the Yan'an Soviet in 1947, the communists dominated most areas of northern China. In 1947, they conquered the major cities of Shenyang and Changchun. The latter, with months-long siege tactics that killed at least 180,000 civilians because, they either starved or got caught between the fronts. As the CCP gains increasingly more ground in China and the troops approach Beijing, Chiang seeks contact with America and Moscow with a request for renewed attempts at mediation. Both no longer see any sense in this, and Mao plainly refuses anyway.

XV. Formation of the People's Republic of China

In 1949, the Red Army conquered Beijing. It is greeted enthusiastically. On the legendary Tiananmen Square, the picture of Chiang is removed and in its place, the portrait of Mao is displayed. The CCP now starts to occupy several cities in a row.

Also in this place, Mao pronounces the founding of the People's Republic of China on October 1, 1949. From this day, the fleeing Chiang Kai-shek is severely persecuted. On December 10, 1949, he escapes to the island of Taiwan. During the Chinese Civil War, between 1927 and 1949, more than 6 million people died according to most estimates.

Chiang is followed by half a million military personnel and around 2 million people who remain loyal to him. Here, he establishes the **Republic of China**, where he becomes president and remains as such until his death in

1975. His supporters make sure that millions worth of art and cultural objects from China are brought to Taiwan. Above all, however, the refugees carry large amounts of money and gold with them, partly from the financial resources of the Kuomintang government. Some of the remaining Kuomintang supporters in China go to Burma and Thailand, others dedicate themselves to the cultivation of opium in the so-called Golden Triangle.

Chiang proclaims the Republic of China as a Chinese government in exile that has full legitimacy. The fronts between him and the mainland CCP become even tougher, especially as no peace treaty is signed. For several years, many Western powers do not recognize the CCP as the legitimate leader of China.

XVI. Mao's Politics

1. Land Reform

Mao Zedong is now **chairman of the Central People's Government**. He won the victory, but takes over a country that is economically unstable and completely exhausted from years of civil war. As the first major political action in 1950, he passes a **law on land reform**. With this, he aims to achieve a fairer distribution of land. He divides the previous social layers in the countryside into **different classes**. Now a distinction is made:

- Large landowners who, themselves, do not work

- Rich farmers who work as well as employ working people and lease parts of their land

- Middle class farmers who own land and farm it themselves

- Poor farmers who own little or no land and have to lease land

- Workers who do not own land, do wage labor and have to live on low incomes

There were whole villages in which one had to wear different colored stripes on one's clothes, indicating which class one belonged to.

As a result of the reform, 60 percent of the rural population took over 40 percent of the agricultural land. But the new landowners faced considerable challenges. They had no adequate knowledge to farm their land and no experience in running a farm.

The result was a stagnation in agricultural productivity, a decline in basic food supply and inflation. The professional handling of cultural goods also changed when the farmers took over the property. As a result, valuable works of art such as ink drawings, ancient manuscripts and antique household items were lost. The Chinese Ministry of Education and Cultural Affairs was forced to confiscate such artifacts for the purpose of preservation.

Under the new Maoist social order, the traditional peasant festivals fell away. They were replaced by party meetings and propaganda events.

2. People's Court

In the land reform, the CCP encouraged peasants to get revenge on the landlords they previously had to suffer.

With this, Mao wanted to bring the farmers over to his side. It led to numerous denunciations. Until the beginning of the 1950s, the number of detentions and executions was estimated at about 2 million people.

There was a procedure which the CCP mandated. The party leaders organized public gatherings in which farmers confronted their former lords, landlords, or employers with their past behavior.

It was a kind of people's court with little formal rules.

Some sessions led to lawsuits, others to immediate punitive measures. Farmers were asked to report extensively on the suffering experienced from abuse to exploitation. Witnesses were neither invited for the indictment or for the accused owner; the accused had little opportunity to voice their justifications. They had to expect insults and beatings, in the worst case, they were killed immediately. Some were sent into exile, others had to give up their private property. Many were forced to do menial labour from there on.

The proceedings played out very differently depending on the area. The sessions were usually highly emotional and dramatic. Reports that the accused forced the prosecutor to pay unaffordable leases, or would take away their entire harvest were not uncommon. Mao saw these gatherings as a necessary step to develop the class consciousness of the peasants and to train them politically.

3. First Five-Year Plan

From 1953 to 1957 Mao carried out his First Five-Year Plan.

He got the concept for this from the Soviet Union, which supported him with a $ 300-million loan, and in addition, sent scientists, technicians and engineers to China.

In fact, this led to success in the industrial development. Steel and coal production increased significantly, surpassing the target figures, and infrastructure also improved. With the good economic growth and much higher wages, the life expectancy of the urban population increased dramatically.

Previously, one did not even reach the age of 40, but could now expect to reach between 55 and 60 years of age.

The communists set up so-called Danweis, which brought many benefits to the working population.

A Danwei was considered a work unit. It was a small community of people where you had your job and also lived.

This way, everyone who worked in the city also had an apartment. It provided creches and partly also schools. In the Danwei, people received their food and medical services and had nursing homes available to them at retirement age. One should identify with it and it was second only to family. But it also exercised strong social control. Whoever wanted to marry, have children or travel, had to communicate with their Danwei first.

The disadvantage of a well-functioning urban industrialization was that it resulted in neglected rural areas. Many people emigrated to the city, and farmers could no longer produce enough food to meet their needs. Mao then resorted to **collectivization**. Much land, which had previously been redistributed, he now made property of the government. By 1957, he had unified over 90 percent of farms to collectives. However, the farmers became more and more dissatisfied, and sometimes attacked the officials responsible for the implementation. At the end of his five-year plan, Mao propagated urban and industrial development as a grandiose success. At the same time, drama was brewing in rural areas.

4. Second Five Year Plan

For the period ranging from 1958 to 1962, Mao called out the second Five-Year Plan. A section of this he called the "Great Leap Forward."

His goal was to advance industrial development, while collectivizing agriculture. All of China should become a society in which the entire life of human beings was based on socialist principles, from birth to death. But Mao wanted too much at once.

The Great Leap changed the situation of the farmers. The people's communes were now a mandatory part of agriculture. If the farming families had previously been forced to make a manageable consolidation, they now had to form communities with up to 300 farm households. This was done under the motto that communism is a paradise, and that people's communes were the way there. Mao did not only have supporters. Some party leaders, such as Zhou Enlai, advised more prudence. But by the end of 1958, according to Mao's order, all agricultural land was divided into about 25,000 people's communes.

The action proceeded disastrously for many farmers. Almost everything that was privately owned was confiscated by government officials. The party transferred agricultural land, buildings, equipment and cattle herds into state ownership.

It became increasingly propaganda intensive, trying to get the people's communes to outdo each other. Towards the end, it absorbed large numbers of private homes and issued the parole that people in the communes should have 6 hours of sleep within 48 hours.

Even in the steel industry, Mao was not satisfied with how fast things were progressing. He wanted to double the remarkably good production to catch up with the much higher industrialized England and keep up with the better developed Soviet Union. That's why he launched a campaign to start building backyard steel furnaces. Everyone should work to melt scrap iron in their backyards and use it to produce everyday objects such as pots. Now, huge clouds of smoke rose up in the cities. This increased the demand for firewood. The resulting products proved to be barely usable. Despite this experience, the government did not stop the process.

Equally, the party's instructions to the peasants were counterproductive, ignoring their decades of experience and knowledge. Measures recommended by an incompetent Soviet agronomist, such as the merging of seeds of different species and the deep plowing of fields, had catastrophic consequences.

When Mao announced his visit to a commune, rice needed to be grown quickly. This gave the impression of a successful harvest. Otherwise, the cultivation of edible food fell victim to much of industrial production and infrastructure construction. The "Great Leap" had failed, but Mao presented his campaign as a great success. However, he did end up calling it off.

Peasants had to deliver a large amount of grain to the government, which was used for redistribution to the cities, but also for export. As a result, at the end of 1959, the rural people's communes no longer had enough for themselves.

This was followed by major natural disasters. There were typhoons and floods as well as heat and drought. The Yellow River overflowed, leaving thousands dead. Diseases occurred en masse. Nevertheless, historians believe that the extreme famine during this and the following two years was mainly caused by Mao's mismanagement.

There was a humanitarian crisis because Mao ignored reality as well as his critics and stuck to his policy.

5. Famine Catastrophe

More and more people were starving in rural areas. In desperation, the farmers ate grass and seeds that they sifted out of animal excrements. Some tried to feed on soil. Then animals like cats, dogs and mice, even rats were eaten. When nothing else could be found, insects were eaten. Women could no longer have children due to extreme malnutrition. At the same time, mental illnesses increased and at least 2 million people committed suicide. Farmers killed their children so they would not have to starve them. But it got even worse.

When people were not able to find anything edible anymore, the only option that remained was cannibalism. Official police reports are documented on this. Some exhumed recently deceased neighbours, others exchanged their children so they would not have to eat their own. Children were abandoned or sold into prostitution.

Then there were **food shortages in the cities**. The government completely blamed this on natural disasters. It did everything to hide the fact there was a famine.

But the misery was not hidden from the International Red Cross, and it offered its help. Mao declined and continued to export grain.

The government made a propaganda film showing healthy people's communes with full granaries. In reality, there were at least 30 million deaths, though some estimates are 50% higher.

6. Social Reforms

Building a new society was the big task Mao had set for himself.

Communism should now determine all living conditions of people, from the economic structure of the country to the individual family.

In practice, this meant transforming a feudal state with rising industrialization into a socialist planned economy and convincing people, shaped by centuries of social tradition, to embrace living together. Socialism should bring equality and justice to all, as quickly as possible. This required a rethinking in the social field. In order to inspire the masses to follow his ideas and to bring about new ways of doing things, Mao launched numerous campaigns to form groups; mainly trade union associations, women's and even children's organizations, and fundamental political participation. Everything was targeted at being democratic. But often, the groups served to spread party propaganda. The democratic reforms were accompanied by political pressure.

Mao initiated far-reaching social reforms. They related to education, attitudes towards religion and the family.

During the dynastic era, more than 80 percent of the population had been illiterate. The mastery of the written language, which consisted of signs, was a privilege of the rich and educated classes. Mao introduces Pinyin writing as the official written language, which is based on the Latin alphabet. This greatly facilitates and accelerates **the literacy of the population**.

A radical social reform was reflected in the marriage law of 1950. Here, rights were established, which gave women in particular more opportunities.

Everyone was now entitled to marry a self-selected partner and decide for themselves where they would like to work. Each spouse had the right to shared property. Divorces were allowed. The law banned polygamy, concubinage, child marriages and the already forbidden, but still practiced, foot binding of women. However, in the rural regions, due to their patriarchal structures, it took generations before the law was fully obeyed.

7. China's constitution

For the first time, the Chinese constitution of 1954 proclaimed the equality of the sexes.

It assured women to have the same rights as men in all areas of political, economic, social, cultural and family life. In addition, measures for maternity leave and childcare were created, making it easier for women to get a job. In reality, it took a long time for gender equality to be fully realized. In the Communist Party itself, men far outnumbered women.

Other reforms affected the equality of all people. Thus, the constitution guarantees all citizens who have reached the age of

18 the right to active and passive voting rights, irrespective of gender, race, nationality, occupation, social origin, education, religion, ownership situations and length of stay.

In terms of sexuality, Maoist China remained puritanical and backwards. Pre-marital sex as well as homosexuality were not allowed. Furthermore, prostitution and sex education in schools fell under the state ban. Sexual scenes were not allowed to occur in films or in books.

In the first half of the twentieth century, supporters of Confucianism and Buddhism were reduced due to the radical changes in China, but many traditional Chinese did not give up their religion. They had great respect for their parents, worshiped their ancestors, cared for their places of burial, and celebrated religious festivals. There were also many followers of the Christian faith as a result of Western missionary activities.

The communist government was anxious to enforce atheism.

It branded religion as an obsolete feudalistic belief. Christian churches and schools were closed, Christian priests and missionaries were severely intimidated. Instead of religious texts, the population should read the writings of Mao and adopt the communist ideology. When Pope Pius XII, like his predecessor, criticized communism in China, the faithful living there were put in even more danger. Two years after the founding of the People's Republic, there were hardly any Christians left in the country because they had fled or been banished.

Under Mao, children were considered equal to their parents and encouraged to feel as committed to the state as their father and mother. In this way, he destroyed the concept of the family as a social unit and the individual's option to withdraw for offspring in the fifties. This culminated in the later Cultural Revolution in that politically active students and soldiers denounced their own parents.

8. National People's Congress

In 1949, after the proclamation of the People's Republic of China, Mao and his party members had formed a government. It was meant to represent the will of all people, though this was impossible due to the enormous differences between the Chinese. One faced a vast mixture of people and classes. In addition to the peasants, there were lords and landowners, remnants of Kuomintang supporters and soldiers, merchants and factories, the remaining warlords and foreign financiers, ethnic minorities and Christians. The constitution was by nature rather provisional.

Several years later, Mao had already initiated a considerable amount of reforms. The new constitution of 1954 contained equal rights legislation and initiated social reforms. It was heavily based on the Soviet model and was meant to set the final victory of socialism in motion. With it, a political system was also instituted.

The National People's Congress was established as a parliamentary organ; it still exists today; it is the world's largest parliament. It usually has 3000 MPs. In 1954, he was elected for the first time.

The goal was that the MPs could represent their province or a subordinate unit. However, a complex voting system did not comply with the representative composition. In addition, literacy in rural areas was not yet advanced enough. The peasants also only knew the CCP because of their ubiquitous mobilizations. When the first People's Congress met, it consisted of 1,226 MPs; including 149 women and 177 ethnic minority representatives.

Mao became president of the People's Republic of China and Zhu De, for many years the senior commander of the Chinese People's Liberation Army, vice president.

In the constitution, there was a dividing line between state and party which was written in simple terms. In reality, how-

ever, the party leadership determined the politics and the MPs agreed. Mao was party chairman and head of state.

The CCP had doubled its membership since 1949. Decisions were made in the Central Committee and the Politburo.

9. Korea War

In 1950, Mao joins the Korean War as he sees it as his duty to support a communist ally. He sends 2 million soldiers who are not officially members of China's state army, but are said to be volunteers. In October, the US conquered the North Korean Pyongyang while the Chinese simultaneously crossed the Yalu River, entering North Korean territory.

The Korean War was a military conflict between North Korea, which after the Second World War had emerged from Soviet occupation, and South Korea, which had emerged from American occupation. It developed into a proxy war between the US and China.

It came to a battle in which the Americans were pushed back. A US general considers using nuclear bombs against China and is laid off by President Truman some time later. The Korean War ended with a ceasefire agreement in 1953 without a winner or loser and without a change of circumstances.

Mao celebrated his participation in the war as a success because his country had opposed the great power of the USA. In fact, the Western powers now considered him to be a serious military strategist and potent communist leader.

But the price was high. After that, China had hundreds of thousands of deaths from the army and the civilian population, as well as high costs from the state treasury. In addition, an initiative of the USA ensured that the People's Republic of China was regarded as an aggressor state.

From 1953 to 1971 for the United Nations (UN), only Taiwan, represented by Chiang Kai-shek, was seen as China. (It was not until 1971 that China was accepted by the UN and replaced Taiwan).

Mao was exposed to international ostracism, isolation and even trade embargos. The relationship with the Soviet Union also deteriorated as Mao felt abandoned by Stalin, who had not given him sufficient support in the Korean War.

XVII. Liu Shaoqi

After Mao's disastrous five-year plan, determined politicians take economic policy into
their own hands.

**Liu Shaoqi, with the help of high-ranking
CCP members; Deng Xiaoping, Zhou Enlai
and Chen Yun, launch reforms that will
improve living conditions.**

In the spring of 1961, Liu visits his home in
Hunan, and in detail, learns about the catastrophic conditions caused by the Great Leap
Forward. He came to the conclusion that the
famine was 30% due to natural disasters and
70% due to human actions - the failure of
politics and thus Mao's government.

While Mao tries to save his face, Liu initiates
changes that he claims to be an adjustment
to Mao's guidelines. He ensures that the regions affected by famine are supplied with
grain, and that grainis no longer exported, but
rather imported to meet demand. He closed

the backyard steel furnaces and instead strengthened the steel industry. He reduced the large people's communes into much smaller units. The farmers got their own plots again, where they were allowed to grow for their own use and sales in markets. They were also allowed to own their own livestock again.

Politically, Liu got the ball rolling too. He rehabilitated intellectuals, artists and unpleasant party members who had previously been condemned, Mao met Liu's activities with incomprehension. He saw this as an obstacle on the way to socialist society.

XVIII. "Learn From" Campaigns

When the economy recovered, the CCP re-launched campaigns. This time, they highlighted exemplary actions that the Chinese people should learn from. In doing so, they skillfully linked the popular Chinese tradition which involved telling stories about heroic young men and women.

In 1963, the communists began with **"Learning from Lei Feng"**. The 21-year-old soldier was killed by a telephone pole while performing his professional duties. The party quoted from his diaries, describing what an honor it was to serve in the People's Liberation Army. Lei became a national hero, whose parents had suffered from their landlords and the Kuomintang, and who with great diligence and unwavering faith in the party had turned to the new China and loyally supported it. Allegedly, he also devoted all his free time to the construction of socialist society, for example by supporting the farmers. But there are big doubts about the validity of this. The fact that such a young person without a high rank left such a large number of personal and official documents, which all agreed with the party is unlikely.

The propaganda machine had started; Mao personally intervened and initiated **"Learning from Daqing".** Here, they had found oil. The promotion of the huge deposit made China independent from oil imports. Daqing, which had suffered from the famine, was now portrayed as a heroic region that had lived up to its civic duty in hard times and had achieved great success with hard work. At the same time, a hero was created, the "Iron Man" Wang. A photo - possibly staged - shows how he uses his full body to jump into a greasy pit to close an uncontrolled source of oil with his own weight.

Mao suffered from loss of power since the failure of the "Great Leap Forward", although he still received great respect. He had to change something.

In 1959, Mao handed over his presidency to Liu Shaoqi, but remained chairman of the CCP.

The reforms of the early 1960s were a turn to capitalism for him. He regarded the persons who carried it as **revisionists**. He took this assessment and terminology from the Soviet Union. In 1966, he decided to counteract the current trend. It was clear to him that he could not shake the economic conditions so as not to worsen the living conditions again. Which is why he turned to culture. He started the **Cultural Revolution** in 1966, and it lasted until 1976.

XIX. Cultural Revolution

Mao had long believed that art and much of science and literature threatened his socialist regime. He urges the Politburo to install a group to study anti-communist attitudes in disciplines such as philosophy, history, law, literature and the arts. When the team sees no need for action, he takes matters into his own hands. First, he wants to prevent the publication of an essay in which he is criticized. When that fails, he puts together his own team, including his wife **Jiang Qing**. They publish dozens of writings attacking anti-socialist works. Mao ensures that the original team is branded as revisionist.

Now, he has crowds of students and scholars backing him. Through intensive propaganda, he achieves them following him fanatically. At 72, he swims in the Yangtze River for a good hour to demonstrate his health and strength, which promotes the revitalization of his power. From his young followers the "**Red Guards**" paramilitary is formed, which already has over one million members in the middle of 1966. He incites them with slogans like "Smash the Old World" to follow his communist ideas.

The young people soon behaved hostile against anyone who was against Mao. In August, Mao appeared in Tiananmen Square to support a Red Guards rally. He showed up in their uniform and talked to members and their leader **Lin Biao** for over 5 hours. He often repeated his presence at their meetings.

Each time he denounced the "Four Olds", namely old customs, old habits, old culture and old ideas.

The Cultural Revolution had noticeably begun. It brought Mao new prestige, but it brought social unrest, fear and restrictions on freedom and possessions to a great deal of the population.

The Red Guards went about it with the impetuosity of youth, coupled with an unwavering belief in communist ideology and Mao as a person. They became more and more radical, first in Beijing, then in other cities. To coat walls of buildings with newspapers was the least. They destroyed what in their eyes, represented China's damnable past. They burned artistic and literary works, destroyed monuments and devastated temples and palaces. Then they started for the people.

Above all, they attacked intellectuals such as professors and teachers, but also priests and nuns, with acts of intimidation as well as physical violence. They plundered and destroyed private homes, giving valuable property to the state. Hundreds of thousands of people lost their homes and savings.

Then they took on influential party members that were critical of Mao. Mao incited them against government members with his slogan "Bomb the headquarters." **Liu Shaoqi and Deng Xiaoping** were attacked with public criticism and malice. Liu was arrested in 1967, one year later, he was deprived of his office and imprisoned. He died in 1969 under harsh prison conditions, including refusal to provide him with essential medicines. Deng first received house arrest and was later exiled.

XX. The Mao Cult

Fueled by Mao himself, the Mao Cult grows ever larger in the course of the Cultural Revolution. He finds the worship of the "right" people good because it mobilizes the masses against oppression, capitalism and imperialism. In this, he includes Marx, Engels, Lenin, Stalin and himself. Mao's portrait is omnipresent in China, from schools and universities to public offices and public places. Even in the private sector, it was interpreted as a sign of rejection, if one did not have a picture of Mao on the walls. Everyone should also have the "Quotations of Chairman Mao Zedong" - often called "Little Red Book" in the West - in a small red book. It was constantly quoted from in schools, universities, factories, people's communes, in the military and others; it was a training text.

Mao was portrayed as the Great Teacher, Great Helmsman or Great Leader. More and more people began to praise his achievements and neglect his mistakes.

There was no talk of the "Big Leap" anymore. Mao portrayed himself as the benevolent and ingenious father of his country and protector of the Chinese people. Socialist art supported the personality cult. Mao's wife, a former actress, personally controlled the development. Artists should emphasize socialist achievements and heroes. Literature, operas and plays were limited to socialist works.

Portraits of Mao were set up in front of public buildings, adorned with flowers and his quotes.

XXI. Down to the Country-side Movement

In 1968, the heyday of the Cultural Revolution was over. Mao and the government issued a new campaign, the movement "Down to the countryside".

Now, young people from the cities should get in close contact with the peasants so that they forgot bourgeois ideas, or would not develop them at all. The future intellectuals should not become critical of the regime. It hit mostly high school graduates and undergraduates, including many who had been under the Red Guards.

The Red Guards found no place in secondary schools and universities, because most had been closed. However, further unrest in the cities by young people was now undesirable. Those who did not voluntarily go to the countryside were forced. For some, the resettlement was a journey with no return.

The adolescents and young adults had no idea what was expected of them. They had been told that they would be enthusiastically received and serve the state because they would support the peasants with revolutionary ideas. They were brought to inland villages and mountain regions.

The peasant population reacted very differently. Above all, the poor people's communes did not appreciate that they had to support more people on their land. The young people from the cities had neither the experience nor the knowledge for agricultural work. The stay on the land became a type of forced labor for many, which they were hardly able to cope with. Some never saw their families in their homeland again. Later, these young people were referred to as **China's Lost Generation**.

XXII. Gang of Four

Until his death, Mao is supported by the so-called **Gang of Four**. The group consists of four Mao followers and his wife Jiang Qing-Madame Mao, as she is often called. They take increasingly more influence on the party and make more and more of their own decisions as Mao gets older and sicker. In order to secure their own power, they discredit Red Guards leader Lin Biao, whom Mao had made deputy party chairman in 1969, and who had become the designated successor as party leader.

In 1971, under mysterious circumstances, Lin dies in a plane crash. It remains unclear whether he had fallen out with Mao and fled or whether he had planned, as officially declared, a coup d'état. In anyway, the Gang of Four uses the situation to strengthen their power. In 1973, Mao gives all four members influential posts in the Politburo. Now Jiang Qing in particular increases his criticism of Lin and links him to his rival Zhou Enlai in order to portray him as a traitor. When Zhou Enlai also dies in 1976, they forbid public memorial ceremonies. The public ignores this and says goodbye to the beloved politician with flowers in Tiananmen Square. In the process, numerous posters are held up against the gang of four. The government has the assembly dissolved and the participants exiled or executed. In the same year Mao dies.

XXIII. Mao's last actions

After the peak of the Cultural Revolution, dissatisfaction and protests against the government arose multiple times. Many CCP members demanded to proceed politically moderate. At the end of the 1960s, there was an action of "self-criticism" within the party again, which in effect meant a purge with violence and humiliation.

In his last years, Mao still brings out more points. The isolation of China from the Western world should come to an end. In 1970, a normalization began inland when the first university reopened. In the same year, China makes a name for itself because it sends its first satellite into space, which is successful. One year later, there is a far-reaching event.

China receives a seat at the United Nations. Another year on, the American President Nixon visits the People's Republic, and of course, Mao personally. This initiates a normalization process.

The formerly hostile Japan also establishes diplomatic relations, and many western states follow suit.

In 1973, Deng Xiaoping is rehabilitated in China. However, a post humous criticism campaign is launched against Lin Bao. The teachings of Confucius, which are still firmly anchored in the people, are also attacked again, so that the for centuries highly revered Confucius is also subjected to a criticism campaign.

Mao's death marks a turning point in the history of modern China. His radical approach is not pursued, at least as far as the economic situation is concerned. The opening to the West also gets driven forward, if only because of the desire to advance Chinese technology. However, the political power of the party should continue to be uninterrupted.

XXIV. Hua Guofeng

Tiananmen Square had been celebrating the founding of the People's Republic of China for years, but after Mao's death, the masses stayed away from the historic place. But those who did come together were the grandees of the party and state leadership, who were fighting for succession. The gang of four got into position, as rival **Hua Guofeng** stepped up.

The adversaries were all followers of Mao, it was only about power.

The Gang of Four and their followers still held the most radical position. Mao's wife had always stood for the merciless oppression of dissidents. A proposal to cooperate with Hua is rejected, they want all the power and at the meeting threaten him with incitement of the masses. At that moment, Hua gets his bodyguards. There is an altercation in which people die. Mao's widow is discharged. The gang of four is neutralized.

Hua sells his own new power position to the population with a trick. He publishes two messages. Firstly, that the corpse of Mao is to be embalmed and made available to the public in a transparent coffin. Secondly, that Mao's entire works will be published under the leadership of the Politburo. Now, it became clear to the Chinese people that Hua, not Mao's widow, was the new leader. Because the person who could dispose of Mao's estate, inevitably had to have power in the state.

XXV. Deng Xioaping

But Deng Xiaoping soon regained a leading position.

From 1978, he was the person in the government who actually made the decisions.

To demonstrate his strength and motivate people to start for great achievements in China, he takes action similar to that of Mao swimming through the Yangtze River. He climbs Huang Shan Mountain at the age of 75.

Deng now makes a policy of domestic moderation and opening of foreign policy. The comments on events in the world are no longer dismissed as greatly capitalist and imperialist machinations.

Deng initiates the "Four Modernizations". They refer to agriculture, national security/defense, industry and advances in science and technology.

Specialists in the field of technology are given preferential treatment. Deng increasingly allows private-sector elements with his new way. Personal wealth was no longer damned. Farmers have been given land and equipment for their own possessions again, and are finally allowed to sell their products in markets and to keep the earnings. Of their produce, such as grains, etc., they must continue to deliver a high, but not intolerable, share to the state.

Deng also promotes industrial production. He allows companies to record their own profits. Now foreign investors are admitted again. In offshore areas, Deng ensures special economic zones where companies from other countries are allowed to settle and even receive tax breaks. In fact, by doing so, he helps China's economy recover and grow. The good results in some provinces should serve as an example for the rest of China. Deng also strengthens the service sector with private-sector incentives.

Through his measures, Deng brings advanced know-how to the country, from which Chinese companies benefit in the medium and long term. Deng travels through the US and gets informed on technological and economic issues.

He also travels to North Korea and informs the communist government about his plans to improve relations with the US and Japan. In 1979, the US and China establish full diplomatic relations. Even with Russia, communications occur diplomatically again, after it had considerable border disputes before. Germany and France become economic partners.

At the end of the 1970s, Deng brought China on the road to a grandiose modernization. At the end of the decade, economic and social change has been brought to life, which lasts permanently.

He describes his initiatives as a process, where one "Crosses the river by feeling the stones." In reality, it means abandoning Mao's radical principles of class struggle and absolute equality. In order to open partially private economies, new laws and regulations that Deng learned from the West are implemented. He also worries about the drastic growth of the population. To stop this, he introduces the **"one-child policy"** (two years later, 2 children are allowed). Only in the cities most parents stick to this policy, while rural families remain trapped in their traditions. Despite the ban on determining the sex of a child before birth, significantly more boys are born in the following years. Female fetuses are aborted en masse, female infants are often abandoned.

Deng continues to rule the CCP and makes sure they have a powerful army. Other parties cannot continue to form, critics are persecuted and silenced. The CCP issues a statement on Mao, in which his policies are judged as 70% good and 30% bad.

A movement that challenges democracy is radically suppressed by arrests. The "wall of democracy", to which critics attach their wall newspapers, is closed. In 1980, Liu Shaoqi is officially rehabilitated, while Hua Guofeng is pushed out of politics and no longer remains in office.

Zhao Ziyang becomes prime minister in 1980 and replaces Hua Guofeng.

He continues to promote the reforms. The Gang of Four is sentenced to high prison terms, the trial takes place in public. Mao's widow receives the death penalty, which is turned into life imprisonment. According to Zhao's conviction, democratic principles must be incorporated into society in order to make economic processes successful.

He thus intensifies the knowledge that China has learned from the enterprises of the western countries. He speaks of the "Preliminary Stage Theory" in order to embed his ideas in socialist ideology. In this way, he sets economic growth in motion that becomes typical for China and still is today.

He also wants to change the political situation. People's representatives at lower levels may now take on several candidates. He wants to realize this at the highest level but cannot enforce this in the party.

Hu Yaobang, a senior official, becomes general secretary in 1982. This post replaces the previous party chairman of the CCP. Hu supports Deng's reform course.

Deng intensifies foreign policy activities. Margaret Thatcher (British Prime Minister) visits China and exchanges views on Hong Kong. In 1983 there is a resumption of diplomatic relations with India. In 1984, China and Britain agree that conditions in Hong Kong would not be fundamentally changed after being handed over to China in 1997 for half a century. But China agrees with the integration of market principles. In 1987, an agreement is made with Portugal on Macau, which is a Portuguese colony until 1999 and then becomes the Special Administrative Region of China.

In 1986 there are student riots and demonstrations. Hua shows tolerance and understanding; in the opinion of the party leadership, he does not approach the critics with enough radicalism. They want to get rid of him.

In early 1987, he loses his position as Secretary General, which Zhao Ziyang now receives.

He will lose it for the same reason.

XXVI. Student's Revolution

The popular Hu Yaobang dies in April 1989. This is followed by weeks of demonstrations of support for him, in which the demand for more democracy increasingly rises.

The demonstrations are initiated by students, but many workers and skilled forces join in. For weeks, they show up in public places, first in Beijing, then in other cities. They stand for fundamental rights that are self-evident in democratic constitutions: freedom of speech, freedom of the press, freedom of assembly and free elections. Nobody gets aggressive, everything runs peacefully and orderly. The organizers ensure that nothing gets out of hand. Hundreds of volunteers provide the demonstrators with free food and medical aid.

These rallies of tens of thousands of people in one place are among the most disciplined events that have ever taken place around the world.

The Beijing Tiananmen Square is occupied for many weeks. Up to 100,000 people can be found here at one time. Many light campfires, dance and sing. Bob Dylan's songs can be heard. The Beijing Symphony Orchestra joins in and plays Beethoven's Ode to Joy. Art students make a copy of New York's Statue of Liberty and position it in direct confrontation with the gigantic Mao portrait. Professors give seminars on the French Revolution and theorists from the era of the European Enlightenment.

In June, students demand a dialogue with the government and the CCP leadership about their concerns. This is rejected. Officials believe that China will not be helped by a democratic social order. In their opinion, which applies before and after this event, China needs a political dictatorship with market-economy elements in order to move the country forward and keep it under control. Several students go on hunger strike to provoke a dialogue.

On the night of June 3 to 4, 1986, the People's Liberation Army moved in with tanks.

Even before they reach the square, there are clashes. The square itself is then cleared by force, as are other meeting places around Beijing. The soldiers use firearms, several thousand peopledie. In the following weeks, hundreds are arrested, many of them executed after a short trial.

Zhao Ziyang had still turned to the students and asked them to stop their action, while Deng and the other officials already prepared for military action.

After the events, Zhao was stripped of his duties and put under house arrest.

XXVII. Jiang Zemin

Jiang Zemin becomes Secretary General of the CCP after Zhao in 1989 and President of the People's Republic four years later.

He defines Marxism-Leninism, Maoism and the economic theories of Deng Xiaoping, as guidelines for the political development of China. During his tenure, the construction of the **Three Gorges Dam**, a dam in the Yangtze River, which includes a hydroelectric power plant, a ship lift and a lock system takes place. This was also set to reduce the risk of flooding caused by the big river. The wattage of the plant is the strongest worldwide.

In the 90s, China's economy continues to develop strongly. Deng travels through southern China, where there are special economic zones as a support measure, and personally promotes the implementation of reforms. Through this, he also wants to tie weaker economic areas to his political ideology. Economic relations with the West continue to develop. In 1991,for example, the first McDonald's restaurant opens in Beijing.

On the foreign policy side, Deng is anxious to further reduce China's isolation. He ensures that the relationship with Japan improves and the relationship with Russia is intensified. He supports mutual economic relations with many countries of the world without staging an international leadership. China is perceived worldwide as a great rising power.

Deng ensures that neighbouring Asian states do not feel threatened by this. He dies in 1997. In the same year, the handover of Hong Kong is carried out according to contract.

In 1998, China is hit by a natural disaster again. The Yangtze and some other rivers overflow from June to September. It is the worst flood in 4 decades with a few thousand deaths and millions of people left homeless. The economic damage was more than $ 20 billion. The People's Liberation Army was almost superhuman in its efforts to save lives, for which the people gave their great gratitude.

In the late 1990s, Jiang Zemin starts **persecuting Falun Gong practitioners**. It is a practice that combines meditative elements with Qigong in order to strengthen health. One believes in spiritual enlightenment.

Jiang sees the supporters as a threat to the system's atheist political tenets, according to which the leadership of the CCP and the government must be supreme authorities. The followers of the movement are persecuted just as religious minorities.

The turn of the millennium brings further openings in domestic and foreign policy.

In 2001, China becomes a member of the important World Trade Organization WTO.

A year later, the CCP announces that it also includes people who are entrepreneurs in their ranks now.

XVIII. Hu Jintao

When Hu Jintao takes over the position of party and state head from Jiang Zemin in 2002, he continues politics seamlessly.

His goal is to move China further into a prosperous society and to advance scientific progress. China's show-piece of space travel also ensues under his reign. In 2003, Yang Liwei starts into space with the Shenzhou 5, where he stays for 21 hours. In the following years, China brings, amongst others, a probe to the moon and develops a space carrier rocket.

For Hu, who is confirmed in his political office in 2007, many problems remain unsolved in the first decade. Taiwan continues to claim exclusive representation for China, although relations with the country also improve. In 2005, many Chinese participate in mass demonstrations against Japan because, amongst others, it should receive a permanent seat on the United Nations Security Council. Many Japanese shops are ravaged. In

the same year, a chemical plant in Jilin ex-
plodes; in addition to 5 deaths, dozens are
injured, and thousands evacuated. The Song-
hua River is heavily contaminated. An earthquake claims 70,000 lives.

**In 2007, journalists reveal a scandal in a
brick factory. Abducted children were
forced to work as slaves, abused and un-
paid.**

Hundreds of fathers had teamed up to look for
their lost sons. Following the liberation of the
children, the police said that they will take
action against trafficking and slavery. The
government announces an action plan in
which it pledges to respect human rights and,
for the first time, acknowledges that it has not
always acted correctly. Another scandal which
concerns thickened milk due to resin materi-
als, which led to severe kidney problems in
infants.

On the positive side, Hu reports that China is
set to host the Olympic Games in 2008 and
will replace Germany in 2009 as world export

champion. In 2010, he can announce the end of the currency bond to the dollar.

On May 1, 2010, seven months after the great celebrations marking the 50th anniversary of the founding of the People's Republic of China, **the Expo 2010 Shanghai China** opens. This was like a symbolic act that China is finally opening up to the world.

Though, a year later, riots start to take place again. Farmers of Wukan Village protest against their officials. They had sold lands to construction companies without involving the tenants.

Residents assumed that politicians had enriched themselves by keeping a good part of the compensation figures to themselves. The farmers demonstrated against the authorities of their village. The state power intervened, there were clashes with the residents and they arrested 13 of them for disturbing public order. One of them died in prisonunder unclear circumstances.

Then the authorities intervened. The farmers were given back land, the arrested were released, and the suspected officials were withdrawn.

For the first time in Chinese history, the municipality has been given the opportunity to freely choose its officials.

Many observers now believed in a democratic breakthrough. But the seizures of land went on, the protest flared up again. Although an official involved was convicted of corruption, rebellious farmers were also arrested and sent to prison.

In 2012, many Chinese join further protests against Japan. They declare the uninhabited **Diaoyu Islands,** the reason which the two nations are fighting, as a Chinese territory.

XXIX. Jinping

In 2012, Xi Jinping becomes the secretary-general of the CCP and becomes president a year later. For years, he has been known for fighting oppositionists and corruption.

With his project **"One belt, one road"** he wants to build a modern Chinese Silk Road. Trade and infrastructure are to be expanded, firstly by land through Central Asia and Turkey to Europe, and secondly by sea via southern Asia and eastern Africa.

In 2013, the Chinese **lunar mission Chang'e 3** lands on the moon. China is the third country in the world to succeed in this mission. In Shanghai, a free trade zone is established. A year later, China is the second largest economy, but also the second largest consumer of fossil fuels. In 2016, as in 2005, the G20 summit takes place in China.

There is still much for China to clarify, for example, the big problem which is **Tibet**. Since

China occupied the "roof of the world", as it is often called, in 1950, conflicts arise again and again. The Chinese destroyed numerous monasteries and temples, the Dalai Lama, as religious leader, had to flee. Remaining farmers were forced to organize themselves into communities. Whether China may claim Tibet as part of the country, is still controversial under international law.

China has conquered a considerable place in the world, far from the former empire. Natural disasters still threaten the country, in 2008,for example, an earthquake claimed about 70,000 lives. There are still regime-critical people who show their dissatisfaction against the party and government. But within a few decades, China has transformed itself from a country with many crises and widespread poverty into an immense economic power with enormous technological knowledge. The world's most populous country has approached Western values in terms of market-based components, but not as far as democracy is concerned.

Copyright and legal notice

This work including all its contents is protected by copyright. Reproduction, in whole or in part, as well as storage, processing, duplication and distribution by means of electronic systems, in whole or in part, is forbidden without the written permission of the Author. All translation Rights reserved.

The contents of this book were searched on the basis of recognized sources and examined with utmost care. However, the Author assumes no guarantee regarding the timeliness, accuracy and completeness of the information provided.

Liability claims against the author relating to the damages of any health, material or ideal nature caused by the use or non-use of the information provided for or by the use of incorrect and incomplete information are in principle excluded, so far, removed from the Author. Intentionally or grossly negligent. This book does not replace medical or professional advice and care.